NFL TODAY

THE STORY OF THE
NEW YORK JETS

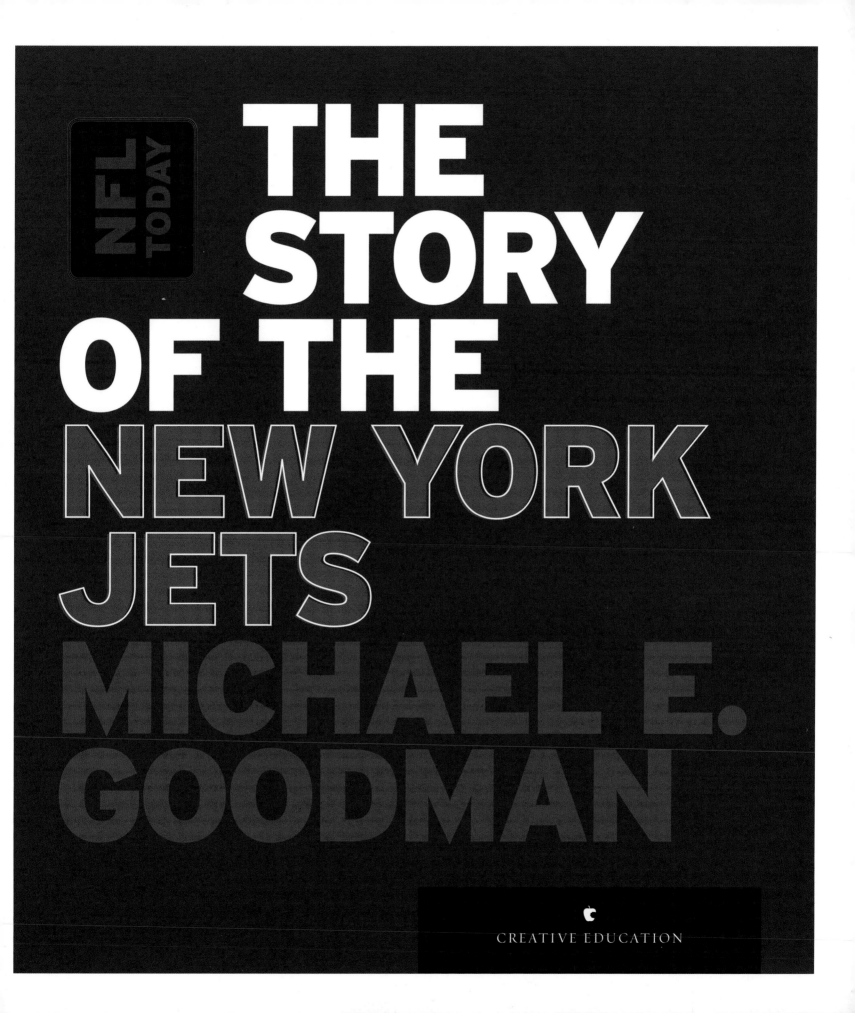

NFL TODAY

THE STORY OF THE NEW YORK JETS

MICHAEL E. GOODMAN

CREATIVE EDUCATION

Cover: Jets offense, 1974 (top), wide receiver
Laveranues Coles (bottom)
Page 2: Wide receiver Justin McCareins
Pages 4–5: 2007 New York Jets
Pages 6–7: Quarterback Joe Namath (left) and
coach Weeb Ewbank (right)

. . . .

Published by Creative Education
P.O. Box 227, Mankato, Minnesota 56002
Creative Education is an imprint of
The Creative Company
www.thecreativecompany.us

Design and production by Blue Design
Design Associate: Sarah Yakawonis
Printed by Corporate Graphics
in the United States of America

Photographs by Corbis (David Bergman, Louie
Psihoyos/Science Faction), Getty Images (Brian
Bahr, Al Bello, Scott Boehm, Tim Clary/AFP, James
Drake/Sports Illustrated, David Drapkin, Stephen
Dunn, Focus On Sport, Bill Hickey/Allsport, Mark
Kauffman//Time & Life Pictures, Nick Laham,
Lonnie Major/Allsport, Vic Milton/NFL, NFL, Darryl
Norenberg/NFL, Al Pereira, Mitchell Reibel/NFL
Photos, Rick Stewart, Kevin Terrell, Rob Tringali/
Sportschrome, Jim Turner/NFL, Lou Witt/NFL)

Library of Congress Cataloging-in-Publication Data

Goodman, Michael E.
The story of the New York Jets / by Michael E.
Goodman.
p. cm. — (NFL today)
Includes index.
ISBN 978-1-58341-805-5
1. New York Jets (Football team)—History—Juvenile
literature. I. Title. II. Series.

GV956.N4G645 2008
796.332'64097471—dc22   2008022712

CPSIA: 020212 PO1534
9 8 7 6 5 4 3

CONTENTS

X

X

ON THE SIDELINES

MEET THE JETS

NEW LEAGUE, NEW TEAM

New York is a city of "mosts." Ever since the first United States census was taken in 1790, New York has ranked as the country's most populous city. It also has the most skyscrapers, the most museums, the most theaters, the most restaurants, the most corporate headquarters, and even the most professional sports teams of any city in America.

New York is also the country's fastest-paced city. Everything moves quickly there—from split-second securities transactions on one of the city's stock exchanges to the rapid maneuvering of a taxi through city traffic. So it is not surprising that one of New York's two franchises in the National Football League (NFL) is named the Jets. That franchise, born in 1960 as the Titans in the American Football League (AFL), quickly gained a reputation for having a wide-open offensive style that was very different from that of the city's older, more conservative football team, the Giants. The highflying Jets built a strong following, particularly among working-class New Yorkers living outside the borough of Manhattan. The loyalty of those fans has never wavered through nearly 50 years of pro football battles.

The Titans were one of the original members of the AFL, a league formed in 1960 to rival the NFL. The team's owner was former broadcaster Harry Wismer, who immediately

X The heavy traffic and 24-hour-a-day bustle of New York, especially through such prominent locations as Times Square, has earned it the nickname "The City That Never Sleeps."

challenged the city's other pro football team by proclaiming, "We're called Titans because titans are bigger than giants."

Playing before sparse crowds in the aging Polo Grounds (where baseball's New York Giants had played before moving to San Francisco in 1958), the Titans posted a respectable 7–7 record their first year. The team featured a potent offense that revolved around the passing of quarterback Al Dorow and the receiving of ends Art Powell and Don Maynard. Maynard became the team's first star. With his outstanding speed and elusive moves, he scored 88 touchdowns during his career (still a club record) and eventually earned a place in the Pro Football Hall of Fame.

Despite Maynard's efforts, the Titans struggled on the field and at the ticket office. By the middle of the 1962 season, Wismer was too broke to pay players' salaries regularly, and he was finally forced to give up the team. A group led by former television executive David "Sonny" Werblin then purchased the franchise for $1 million.

Werblin gave the club a complete makeover, changing its name from the Titans to the peppier-sounding Jets and replacing the players' drab blue-and-gold uniforms with brighter kelly-green-and-white ones. Then he brought in veteran coach Weeb Ewbank to reshape the team's roster and

DON MAYNARD

WIDE RECEIVER
TITANS/JETS SEASONS: 1960-72
HEIGHT: 6 FEET
WEIGHT: 180 POUNDS

When Coach Sammy Baugh was putting together the first roster for the New York Titans in 1960, he remembered fellow Texan Don Maynard, a fleet-footed receiver then playing football in Canada. Baugh convinced team owner Harry Wismer to sign Maynard to the team's first contract. For the next 13 years, Maynard would play a vital role in the New York offense. During 5 of those seasons, he caught 50 or more passes for more than 1,000 yards each year. Maynard was renowned for his ability to improvise on the field. He would find a way to get open, even in the tightest coverage. Then he would use his outstanding speed to catch up with tosses from the team's quarterback. Once Joe Namath joined the Jets in 1965, the Namath-to-Maynard combination became one of the most lethal in the AFL. The pair clicked for two touchdowns in the AFL Championship Game in 1968, including the game winner. When Maynard retired in 1973, he held the pro football records for career catches and receiving yards.

TITAN-IC TROUBLES

When the AFL was established in 1960, most of the owners were wealthy businessmen. That was not true of Titans owner Harry Wismer, however. Wismer was a fast-talking sports broadcaster who was known for stretching the truth at times. He put most of his life's savings into buying the team in hopes of turning a quick profit if the new league was a success. The league and the New York franchise eventually succeeded but not while Wismer was involved. During the three years Wismer owned the Titans, the team was a financial bust. The club had to scrounge for practice fields and played its home games before tiny crowds in the decaying Polo Grounds. To cut down on expenses, Wismer stopped paying most of the bills, including hotel tabs and salary checks. Frustrated players finally took a stand in 1962, refusing to board the plane for an away game in Denver unless their salaries were guaranteed. Lamar Hunt, another AFL owner, paid the salaries, and the league took over the Titans to ensure that the AFL kept a team in New York.

playbook. Ewbank, who had previously led the Baltimore Colts to two NFL championships, was soft-spoken and didn't try to fire up players by yelling at them. "Weeb Ewbank treated us like men, and I appreciated that," recalled former Jets center John Schmitt.

espite their losing record in 1963 (5–8–1), Coach Ewbank's Jets began winning more fan support in New York. The fans had even more to cheer about the next season when the team moved to a new home—Shea Stadium in the New York City borough of Queens—and featured a new star, running back Matt Snell, the 1964 AFL Rookie of the Year.

The excitement reached a fever pitch in 1965 when flashy quarterback Joe Namath arrived in New York from the University of Alabama. Werblin had convinced Namath to join the AFL instead of the NFL by offering him a three-year contract for the amazing sum of $427,000. This made Namath the highest-paid American athlete in any sport. With his good looks and cocky attitude, Namath became a star both on the field and off it, and sportswriters nicknamed him "Broadway Joe."

Namath's teammates weren't jealous of the money he made or the publicity he received. Instead, they were impressed by his work ethic. "He paid the price," said

Known as one of the strongest pound-for-pound players in the AFL, running back Emerson Boozer spent his entire 10-year pro career with the Jets, scoring 64 total touchdowns. X

Maynard. "He worked just as hard and studied just as much film as anybody else. In that way, naturally, you accept the guy for what he does. He comes to play, and he comes to win."

Broadway Joe quickly proved that he was worth every penny of his big contract. In 1966, he led the Jets to a 6–6–2 record by throwing long bombs to Maynard and second-year receiver George Sauer Jr. Everything was looking bright for the Jets until Namath began struggling with knee problems.

Namath played through the pain the next year, leading the Jets to their first winning record (8–5–1) and becoming the first quarterback in either the AFL or NFL to pass for more than 4,000 yards in a season. Sauer and Maynard were also outstanding in 1967, as was rookie running back Emerson Boozer, who paired with Snell to give New York perhaps the AFL's best rushing duo. The Jets were ready to soar.

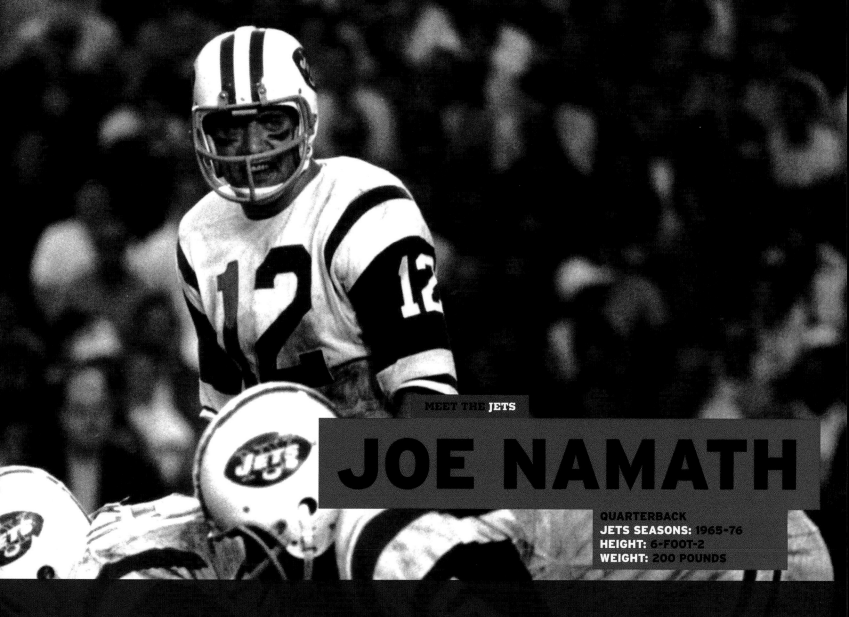

JOE NAMATH

QUARTERBACK
JETS SEASONS: 1965-76
HEIGHT: 6-FOOT-2
WEIGHT: 200 POUNDS

Legendary University of Alabama coach Bear Bryant called Joe Namath "the greatest athlete I've ever coached," and later Jets owner Woody Johnson called him "the most important player in the history of this franchise." Namath was not only a football star, he was also a league maker. Namath's decision to sign with the Jets instead of the NFL's St. Louis (now Arizona) Cardinals in 1965 brought the AFL a credibility it had not achieved before with sportswriters or fans. Soon, New York fans packed Shea Stadium for Jets games, the local press expanded its coverage of the AFL, and television ratings for AFL contests soared. When Namath upheld his guarantee of victory in Super Bowl III, NFL owners began to see the economic value of merging the two leagues. On the field, Namath had a lightning-quick delivery and a cannon arm. "He could throw a ball through a wall," said Jets center John Schmitt. Off the field, he was treated as a celebrity and was once paid $10,000 to shave off his mustache for a shaving cream commercial.

NAMATH KEEPS HIS PROMISE

X -

Jets fans had high expectations in 1968. The club had the league's top quarterback directing one of the AFL's best offenses, as well as a great defense led by end Gerry Philbin, linebacker Al Atkinson, and cornerback Johnny Sample. The Jets rolled over opponents, finishing with an 11–3 record to top the Eastern Division of the AFL and earn a berth in the AFL Championship Game against the Oakland Raiders.

In a tight battle at Shea Stadium, New York edged out Oakland 27–23, thanks to three Namath touchdown passes and two field goals by kicker Jim Turner. Namath didn't even remember much of that game, though, after he suffered a concussion in the second quarter. Still, he was able to rally the Jets, leading a late fourth-quarter drive for the winning touchdown.

The next stop on the "Jets Express" was Miami, where New York would face the NFL champion Baltimore Colts in Super Bowl III. That Super Bowl was a turning point in professional football history. It was more than just a game between two teams—it also represented a war between two leagues. Only die-hard New York or AFL fans believed the Jets had any chance of beating the Colts. After all, the AFL champs that played in Super Bowls I and II had been demolished by the Green Bay Packers of the NFL, and the Colts featured such

X Joe Namath was a New York icon before the 1968 season; after it, Broadway Joe became one of the greatest celebrities in all of sports, hounded by both fans and reporters.

X With Don Maynard (number 13) hampered by injury, fellow receiver George Sauer posted 133 receiving yards in Super Bowl III.

future Hall-of-Famers as quarterback Johnny Unitas and tight end John Mackey. Before the contest, some writers predicted that the powerful Colts would win by as much as 30 points. Namath had other ideas, though. "Our team is better than any NFL team," he announced boldly. "We're going to win Sunday. In fact, I guarantee it."

Coach Ewbank was upset when he learned of Namath's guarantee. "You can't go talking like this and giving the Colts

X The Jets defense rose to the challenge in Super Bowl III, keeping the high-powered Colts out of the end zone until the fourth quarter.

THE HEIDI GAME

The Jets' 1968 season featured not only an unexpected Super Bowl victory but also two remarkable games against the Oakland Raiders. The Jets won the more important contest—a come-from-behind victory in the AFL Championship Game. However, an earlier game that they lost became even more famous. The game took place in Oakland but drew a large television audience in New York. The lead seesawed back and forth until, with 65 seconds to go (and at nearly 7:00 P.M. in the East), New York's Jim Turner kicked what seemed to be the winning field goal. At least that's what Jets fans thought; they never got to see the game's final minute. Because the television network broadcasting the game had previously committed to show the family film *Heidi* at 7:00 P.M., it cut away from the game on the East Coast. New Yorkers never saw Oakland stun the Jets with two lightning-quick touchdowns to win 43–32. Outraged fans bombarded their local stations with calls. In a nationwide poll taken years later, football fans voted "The Heidi Game" as one of the all-time most memorable games.

fuel," he told his star. But Namath's words charged up his own teammates more than the Colts. On Super Sunday, millions of football fans watched in disbelief as New York dominated the game. The Jets scored first on a Snell touchdown run, and their defense refused to budge throughout the game. The 16–7 Jets win was one of the most shocking upsets in sports history. It also proved that AFL teams could be competitive with NFL teams and helped pave the way for a successful merger of the two leagues before the 1970 season.

ollowing the Super Bowl win, Jets fans began to talk about a dynasty. They were confident that Namath's arm could carry them to more titles. Unfortunately, Broadway Joe's battered knees and serious injuries to other team leaders quickly grounded the Jets.

After joining the NFL in 1970, the Jets settled near the middle of the American Football Conference (AFC) standings. Namath remained a fine passer, and receiver Jerome Barkum and flamboyant running back John Riggins added power to the offense. But the club's record continued to slide.

When the Jets won a total of only six games over the course of the 1975 and 1976 seasons, the team's owners started making changes. First, a new coach—former Cleveland Browns linebacker Walt Michaels—was brought in. Then Michaels turned the offense over to young quarterback Richard Todd and released Namath. Jets fans bid a sad farewell to Broadway Joe, who ended his New York career having amassed more than 27,000 passing yards and 170 touchdowns—club records that still stand today.

X John Riggins would go on to greater fame with the Washington Redskins, but he got his start as a steamrolling fullback with the Jets.

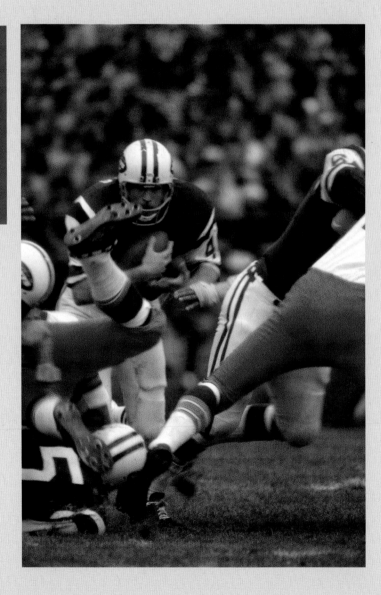

MARK GASTINEAU

DEFENSIVE END
JETS SEASONS: 1979-88
HEIGHT: 6-FOOT-5
WEIGHT: 275 POUNDS

Mark Gastineau was a huge man, but he was also amazingly quick and strong. He could do a squat lift with a 700-pound barbell on his shoulders and run a 40-yard dash in 4.8 seconds. With his combination of speed and aggressiveness, Gastineau, as part of "The New York Sack Exchange," helped make the quarterback sack one of the most exciting defensive plays in football. But smashing through a wall of blockers to get to the quarterback was never enough for Gastineau; he usually took it one step further by performing a twirling dance over his fallen opponent. The dance excited Jets fans but infuriated opposing players and fans. "I don't hurt anybody with it," he once protested. "It's just me." Despite all of his talent, Gastineau was always a little bit too wild. He got into trouble several times off the field and shortened his football career by abusing steroids and other drugs. Still, for the 10 years he spent in New York, he brought an intensity to the Jets defense that helped drive the team to the top of the AFC.

DISAPPOINTMENTS AND DEFEAT

Coach Michaels's Jets, featuring Todd and defensive ends Joe Klecko and Mark Gastineau, began revving up crowds at Shea Stadium in the late 1970s. Klecko and Gastineau joined with defensive tackles Marty Lyons and Abdul Salaam to form a hard-rushing defensive line that sportswriters labeled "The New York Sack Exchange." Gastineau earned both cheers and jeers when he celebrated his sacks by doing a dance over the fallen quarterback. Outraged owners of other NFL teams soon passed the "Gastineau Rule" to outlaw such showy celebrations after a sack.

In 1981, the Jets reached the NFL playoffs for the first time. In the opening round, the Jets fell behind the Buffalo Bills 24–0, made a remarkable comeback, but then lost 31–27. Coach Michaels wasn't discouraged, however. "If all of New York hasn't fallen in love with this team yet," he said, "then they will in 1982."

The 1982 Jets advanced all the way to the AFC Championship Game, where they lost to the Miami Dolphins

End Mark Gastineau (left) and tackle Marty Lyons (right) played together with the Jets for 10 seasons, making up half of "The New York Sack Exchange." X

JOE KLECKO

DEFENSIVE TACKLE/END
JETS SEASONS: 1977-87
HEIGHT: 6-FOOT-3
WEIGHT: 263 POUNDS

Joe Klecko developed a special bond with Jets fans because, like many of them, he came from a working-class background. Klecko had worked as a truck driver and a boxer before attending Philadelphia's Temple University and starring on its football team. Because NFL scouts didn't regard Temple as a football powerhouse, Klecko was only a sixth-round pick in the 1977 NFL Draft. But he showed Jets coaches his talent as a pass rusher right away and was a starter at defensive end by the ninth game of his rookie season. Opposing blockers quickly grew to respect Klecko's strength and skills. Seattle Seahawks center Blair Bush said, "When Joe slams into you, we call it 'The Klecko Skate' because when he hits you, it looks like you're rolling backwards on skates." One of the most versatile defensive stars of all time, Klecko was the first player ever elected to the Pro Bowl at three different positions—defensive tackle, defensive end, and nose tackle. In 2004, Klecko joined Don Maynard and Joe Namath as the only Jets stars to have their numbers retired.

14–0 on a muddy field in Miami's Orange Bowl. Michaels retired after the loss and was replaced by new coach Joe Walton. That was only one major change for the Jets. Before the 1984 season, the club also moved its home base across the Hudson River to Giants Stadium (which Jets players and fans preferred to call "the Meadowlands"). Jets fans found their way to New Jersey and filled the larger stadium with even louder shouts of "J–E–T–S! Jets! Jets! Jets!"

The loudest cheers were reserved for quarterback Ken O'Brien, halfback Freeman McNeil, and wide receiver Al Toon, who led the club back to the playoffs in 1985. Fans became even more excited in 1986, when the Jets got off to a 10–1 start. Then O'Brien, Klecko, and several other key players went down with injuries, and the Jets lost their final five regular-season games, limping into the playoffs. They made a great showing in the postseason, however, first defeating the Kansas City Chiefs behind substitute quarterback Pat Ryan and then taking the Cleveland Browns into double-overtime before losing a hard-fought game. But Jets fans were left disappointed again.

Then the Jets seemed to lose their winning touch and slipped down the AFC standings for the rest of the decade. Even the outstanding efforts of Pro-Bowlers such as safety

Steady kicker Pat Leahy wore Jets green from 1974 to 1991, playing until the age of 40 and becoming the franchise's all-time scoring leader with 1,470 total points. **X**

Erik McMillan and tight end Mickey Shuler weren't enough to halt the team's negative slide. After a miserable 4–12 season in 1989, Walton was fired, and a new rebuilding process began.

The Jets made it back to the playoffs in 1991, thanks in large part to the efforts of record-setting placekicker Pat Leahy. Then the club took a nosedive in the two seasons that followed. After another losing campaign in 1994, team owner Leon Hess announced, "I'm 80 years old, and I want results

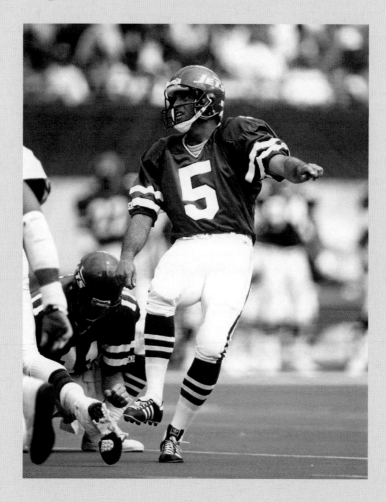

NAMATH'S BOOTLEG

Joe Namath's guarantee before Super Bowl III was not his only daring prediction during his Jets career. He made another bold one midway through the 1974 season. The Jets were 1–7, and Namath's ailing knees were causing him to have a miserable year. Still, "Broadway Joe" predicted that the team would win its final six games and finish at .500. Amazingly, that is what the Jets did, beginning with an overtime victory against the New York Giants. That game featured one of the most unforgettable plays in team history. Trailing 20–13 late in the fourth quarter, the Jets had the ball on the Giants' three-yard line. Namath called a running play for halfback Emerson Boozer, but at the last second he surprised everyone by faking to Boozer and taking the ball himself in a stiff-legged bootleg to the left. Just as he limped across the goal line, two Giants players closed in, but Namath raised his arm as if to say, "Don't touch me," and the defenders held back. A few minutes later, the Jets won the game in overtime to start their six-game winning streak.

now. I'm entitled to some enjoyment from this team, and that means winning."

Hess then made a disastrous decision, turning the club over to former NFL tight end Rich Kotite, who had recently been fired as coach of the Philadelphia Eagles. The easygoing Kotite had trouble enforcing his rules on players, and the Jets plummeted to a 3–13 record in 1995. "This is about as bad as you're ever going to see," Kotite remarked at the end of the season, but he was wrong. The next year, the club managed to win only one game. Kotite was sent packing and replaced by a man who knew a lot about winning in Giants Stadium, former New York Giants coach Bill Parcells.

X   Nicknamed "The Big Tuna," Bill Parcells came to the Jets in 1997 with a reputation as a no-nonsense leader and a resumé that included two NFL Coach of the Year awards.

X   The mid-1990s were rough times for the Jets; in 1995, quarterback Bubby Brister and his teammates failed to score more than 10 points in 7 of their 16 games.

BUILDING A WINNER

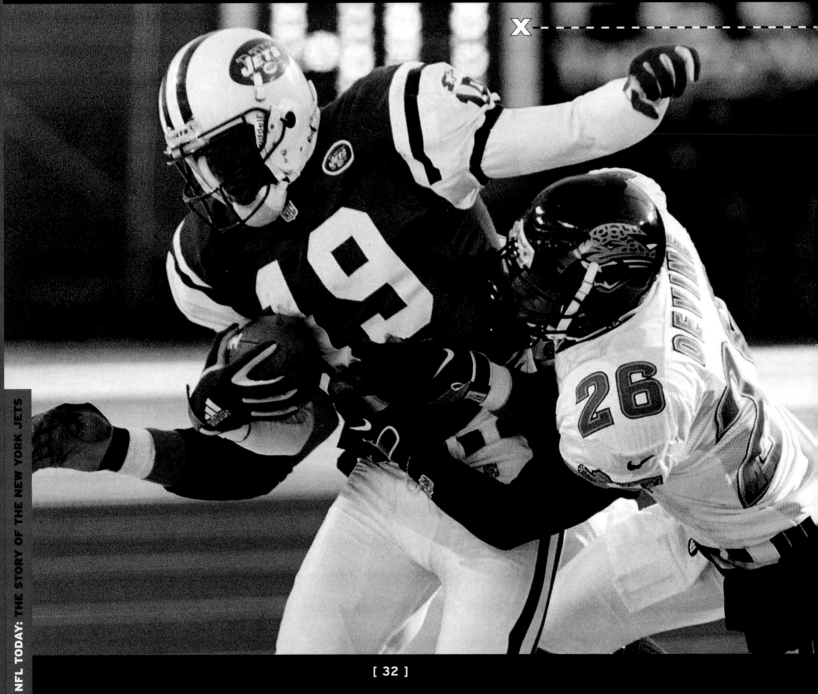

X-------------------

The name "Bill Parcells" was legendary in New York. A native
of northern New Jersey, Parcells had coached the Giants from
1983 to 1990 and had led them to Super Bowl victories in
1986 and 1990. After a three-year attempt at retirement, he
returned to the game and transformed a broken-down New
England Patriots team into a Super Bowl contender. Now, Hess
offered Parcells a new challenge back in New York.

Parcells's Jets lineup featured two key offensive weapons:
receivers Wayne Chrebet and Keyshawn Johnson. The two
were as different as night and day. The 5-foot-10 Chrebet
was quiet, steady, and tough—more of a hard worker than a
natural athlete. At 6-foot-4, Johnson was taller and smoother
than Chrebet. He was also talkative and flashy. Together, they
formed a potent receiving duo.

To improve the team's chances, Parcells signed three free
agents—running back Curtis Martin, center Kevin Mawae, and
quarterback Vinny Testaverde. The new arrivals helped turn

Under Coach Parcells's magic touch, the Jets jumped from a
1–15 record in 1996 to 9–7 in 1997. The coach then promised his
players that more and better changes were ahead. "I told them
that nobody could stand still," he later recalled. "You either get
better, or you get worse. It's that simple."

To improve the team's chances, Parcells signed three free
agents—running back Curtis Martin, center Kevin Mawae, and
quarterback Vinny Testaverde. The new arrivals helped turn

WAYNE CHREBET

WIDE RECEIVER
JETS SEASONS: 1995-2005
HEIGHT: 5-FOOT-10
WEIGHT: 188 POUNDS

Wayne Chrebet had everything going against him when he asked the Jets for a tryout during the summer of 1995. He was smaller than most professional wide receivers, had played at tiny Hofstra University on New York's Long Island, and had not been drafted by any pro team. In fact, when Chrebet showed up for his first Jets workout, the team's security guard didn't want to let him in. But what Chrebet had going for him was his incredible courage: He was not afraid to run pass routes across the middle of the field where larger defensive players might plow into him to try to dislodge the ball from his hands. Amazingly, Chrebet not only made the team in 1995 but became one of its offensive stars for 11 seasons. By the time he was forced to retire after suffering a series of concussions, Chrebet ranked second in the Jets' record book in receptions, third in receiving yards, and third in touchdown passes caught. A favorite in New York, scores of fans showed up to games wearing his number 80 jersey.

the Jets into an offensive powerhouse in 1998 and led the
club to its first division title since its AFL days in 1969.

In the playoffs, the Jets defeated the Jacksonville Jaguars
34–24 to reach the AFC Championship Game against the
Denver Broncos, the defending Super Bowl champs. But in the
title contest, Denver capitalized on six New York turnovers to
crush the Jets' Super Bowl dreams 23–10.

Parcells stepped down after the 1999 season and handed
the coaching reins to his former assistant, Al Groh. Groh
led the Jets for only one year before resigning to become a
college coach, but he made a key move that would brighten
the club's future, selecting quarterback Chad Pennington in
the first round of the 2000 NFL Draft.

X A Pro-Bowler
every year from 1999
to 2004, Kevin Mawae
was widely regarded
as the best center
in the NFL during his
prime years.

At Marshall University, Pennington had been both an athletic and academic All-American. The Jets were impressed with Pennington's accurate throwing arm, his commanding size (at 6-foot-3 and 225 pounds), and his intelligence. Pennington sat on the Jets bench for two years until new coach Herm Edwards inserted the young passer into the starting lineup midway through the 2002 season.

Under Pennington, the Jets rebounded from an upsetting 2–5 start to finish the year as AFC East Division champs with a 9–7 record, putting them in the postseason again. The young quarterback led the NFL in passer rating, a measure of passing accuracy and performance. Pennington's poise under fire impressed fans, coaches, and teammates. "Chad is like a coach on the field," said Jets tight end Anthony Becht. "He understands everything. He knows what has to be done in every situation."

Optimism was high in the Meadowlands before the 2003 season. Then, in a preseason exhibition game against the Giants, Pennington was slammed to the ground, shattering his wrist. By the time he returned two months later, the Jets were in last place in the AFC East and doomed to suffer another losing season. Fans began to wonder if better times could be ahead.

FIREMAN ED

Every NFL team has its special fans, and many have cheerleaders. But the Jets have both in one person—"Fireman Ed" Anzalone. Ever since the Jets moved to the Meadowlands in 1984, Anzalone has led the crowds in chanting, "J-E-T-S, Jets! Jets! Jets!" numerous times each game. He does his cheerleading perched on the shoulders of another "superfan" while wearing a number 42 Jets jersey (in honor of former running back Bruce Harper) and a green fireman's helmet similar to the one he wears on the job as a New York City firefighter. The first time he led the chant, Anzalone tried standing on the front-row railing so he could be seen. But when he nearly toppled over, his brother put him on his shoulders. Within a few games, Fireman Ed had at least 5,000 fans chanting along with him. Soon, the entire stadium began rocking with the cheer. "I feel I make a difference," Anzalone once told reporters. "Seventy-six thousand fans give me the opportunity each week to

MANGINI MAGIC

In 2004, Pennington, now fully recovered and re-energized, directed the Jets to a 5–0 start by utilizing a "West Coast" offense that featured short passes down the field to receivers Justin McCareins and Santana Moss and slashing runs by Curtis Martin. The defense, led by rookie linebacker Jonathan Vilma, was even more impressive, giving up an average of only 16 points per game. The Jets finished the year 10–6 and qualified for the playoffs.

The Jets' postseason adventure featured two 20–17 overtime contests. New York won the first, defeating the San Diego Chargers on a Doug Brien field goal in the extra session. The following week, the team traveled to Pittsburgh to take on the powerful Steelers and nearly won that game as well. But the Steelers rallied to tie the contest 17–17 late in the fourth quarter and won it on an overtime field goal. After the game, reporters asked Coach Edwards if he was satisfied with how his club had rebounded from its last-place finish the previous year. "We're excited, but we're not satisfied," he said. "No, no, we won't be satisfied until we win the championship."

The club's championship dreams quickly faded the next year, however, when both Pennington and backup quarterback Jay Fiedler suffered shoulder injuries in the third game of the season. Then Martin went down with a knee injury that effectively ended not only all hopes for the Jets that season but also the career of one of the NFL's all-time leading rushers.

Following the season, Jets management decided to go in an entirely new direction, replacing Edwards with 35-year-old Eric Mangini, who had spent the previous few seasons as a defensive coach for the New England Patriots. Now he was taking over the reins of the Patriots' biggest rival. "I know how passionate the Jets fans are," Mangini said as he took the job. "I've been here with them and I've played against them, and I'm a lot happier to be here with them."

No one expected the Jets to go far under their rookie coach in 2006, but Mangini brought a new fire to the Meadowlands, inspiring the team to a solid 10–6 record. Some writers referred to the new winning spirit in New York as "Mangini Magic." The most magical game of the season took place on a rainy November Sunday, when Mangini's Jets

LEARNING TO WALK AGAIN

At 6-foot-5 and 275 pounds, defensive end Dennis Byrd was big and powerful. He seemed destined for NFL stardom until November 29, 1992, when his career came to a crashing halt. Playing against the Kansas City Chiefs at the Meadowlands, Byrd and fellow defensive end Scott Mersereau rushed Chiefs quarterback Dave Krieg from opposite sides. When Krieg slid forward, the two defenders collided, and Byrd slammed his helmet into Mersereau's chest. While the fans stood stunned, Jets trainers stabilized Byrd's broken neck before putting him on a stretcher, probably saving his life. For the next week, Byrd lay in a hospital, totally paralyzed. Then doctors noticed a slight movement in his big toe. The good news was relayed to Jets players before the start of their next game against the Buffalo Bills. They responded with a 24–17 upset win and later delivered the game ball to Byrd's hospital room. Through months of hard work, Byrd learned to walk again. Following his recovery, Byrd established a camp near his home in Oklahoma to help improve the lives of physically challenged children.

TRIPLE OVERTIME

Jets players gave new meaning to the term "working overtime" in 2004. It all began in the final game of the regular season against the St. Louis Rams, when Jets kicker Doug Brien connected on a last-second field goal to send the contest into overtime. The Jets lost that day on a Rams field goal in the extra period, but they had better luck the following week in a first-round playoff game against the San Diego Chargers. That game, too, went into overtime after the Jets blew a 10-point fourth-quarter lead. New York then survived a Chargers drive in the extra period before quarterback Chad Pennington led the Jets down the field to set up a game-winning Brien kick. It was the first time the Jets had won a playoff game away from the Meadowlands in 22 years. Playing the Pittsburgh Steelers the following week, the Jets once again faced sudden death in overtime. This time they came up short, putting an end to their season. No NFL team had ever played three consecutive overtime games before, nor put its fans through so much tension.

stunned his former team, the Patriots, 17–14. The two teams

met again during the 2006 playoffs, with the Pats winning

that time, 37–16. Despite the loss, Mangini and the Jets felt

that they had made an important statement—that the club

was definitely moving upward again.

Even after a subpar year of winning only four games in

2007, mostly as a result of injuries to key players, optimism

remained high in the Meadowlands. That optimism grew just

before the start of the 2008 season when the Jets obtained

future Hall-of-Famer Brett Favre in a trade with the Green

Bay Packers. The 38-year-old quarterback proved that he still

had his winning touch as he slung the ball around the field

X Coach Eric Mangini's 10–6 record in his first season in New York had excited Jets fans calling him "Man-Genius," but the team fell to 4–12 the next year.

X Although best known for his accurate passing, quarterback Chad Pennington managed to score six rushing touchdowns for the Jets, too.

CURTIS MARTIN

RUNNING BACK
JETS SEASONS: 1998–2005
HEIGHT: 5-FOOT-11
WEIGHT: 210 POUNDS

Growing up in Pittsburgh, Pennsylvania, Curtis Martin never dreamed of playing professional football. In fact, he didn't even join his high school team until his senior year, when his mother insisted he take part in a school activity to keep him out of trouble. Martin quickly proved that he had the talent to succeed as a college running back at the University of Pittsburgh and then as a pro with the New England Patriots under coach Bill Parcells. In 1998, one year after Parcells moved on to the Jets, he brought Martin to New York. Signing Martin cost the Jets two high draft picks, but Parcells said, "He's worth twice the price." Martin topped the 1,000-yard mark each of the next 7 seasons with the Jets and led the NFL in rushing in 2004. Despite his success, Martin was always humble and even-tempered. Jets offensive coordinator Paul Hackett called him "the quiet superstar." He was also a very generous person, donating more than 10 percent of his earnings to a foundation he formed to help people who were homeless or jobless.

to receivers Laveranues Coles and Jerricho Cotchery. Thanks to their efforts and those of such players as running back Thomas Jones and cornerback Darrelle Revis, the Jets won five straight games at midseason to go 8–3. Unfortunately, Favre and his teammates then fell out of sync, and New York dropped four of its last five games—a disappointing losing skid that knocked the Jets from playoff contention and prompted team owners to fire Coach Mangini.

The history of the New York Jets includes the highest highs and the lowest lows, but today's team seems to have at last reached cruising altitude near the top of the AFC. After celebrating one Super Bowl victory and then enduring many forgettable seasons, Jets fans throughout the New York metropolitan area are looking forward to the day when green and white are the colors of an NFL champion once more.

Arriving in 2008, veteran quarterback Brett Favre fired six touchdown passes in one early-season game—tying the Jets' team record. X

INDEX